50 Classic Recipes with a Modern Twist

By: Kelly Johnson

Table of Contents

- Truffle Mac and Cheese
- Kale Caesar Salad with Parmesan Crisps
- Avocado Toast with Poached Egg and Pesto
- Lobster Roll with Spicy Sriracha Mayo
- BBQ Pulled Pork Tacos with Pineapple Salsa
- Kimchi Grilled Cheese Sandwich
- Bison Burgers with Blue Cheese
- Sweet Potato Fries with Chipotle Aioli
- Cauliflower Crust Pizza with Arugula
- Miso-Glazed Salmon with Quinoa
- Buffalo Cauliflower Wings
- Pumpkin-Spiced French Toast
- Spaghetti Carbonara with Zucchini Noodles
- Vegan Chocolate Avocado Mousse
- Coconut Milk Pancakes
- Tuna Poke Bowl with Brown Rice
- Spinach Artichoke Dip with Roasted Red Peppers
- Duck Confit Tacos with Mango Salsa
- Sweet and Spicy Korean Fried Chicken
- Lamb Meatballs with Mint Yogurt Sauce
- Chickpea Pasta with Roasted Vegetables
- Charred Brussels Sprouts with Balsamic Glaze
- Sriracha Honey Roasted Carrots
- Gourmet Grilled Cheese with Apple Slices
- Sous Vide Steak with Chimichurri
- Greek Yogurt Parfait with Granola and Fresh Berries
- Quinoa-Stuffed Bell Peppers
- Crispy Duck Breast with Orange Glaze
- Tiramisu Ice Cream Sandwiches
- Spaghetti Squash Alfredo

- Grilled Corn Salad with Feta and Lime
- Matcha Green Tea Cheesecake
- Shrimp Scampi with Zoodles
- Slow-Cooked Short Ribs with Gremolata
- Tomato Soup with Grilled Cheese Croutons
- Sourdough Pizza with Prosciutto and Arugula
- Chili Lime Roasted Chickpeas
- Eggplant Parmesan with Mozzarella and Pesto
- Crab Cakes with Avocado-Lime Sauce
- Avocado Chocolate Chip Cookies
- Grilled Watermelon Salad with Feta
- Gluten-Free Banana Bread with Almond Flour
- Spicy Thai Peanut Noodles
- Lobster Mac and Cheese
- Smoked Salmon Eggs Benedict on Sweet Potato Toast
- Buffalo Chicken Stuffed Sweet Potatoes
- Lemon Ricotta Pancakes with Berries
- Grilled Portobello Mushroom Burgers
- Roasted Cauliflower Steaks with Chimichurri
- Chocolate Chip Skillet Cookie with Sea Salt

Truffle Mac and Cheese

Ingredients:

- 2 cups elbow macaroni
- 2 tablespoons butter
- 2 tablespoons all-purpose flour
- 2 cups whole milk
- 1 ½ cups sharp cheddar cheese, shredded
- ½ cup Parmesan cheese, grated
- 2 tablespoons truffle oil
- Salt and pepper to taste
- 1/4 cup breadcrumbs (optional for topping)

Instructions:

1. **Cook the Pasta:** Cook macaroni according to package instructions. Drain and set aside.
2. **Make the Cheese Sauce:** In a saucepan, melt butter over medium heat. Whisk in flour and cook for 1-2 minutes. Gradually add milk while whisking continuously. Cook until thickened.
3. **Add the Cheese and Truffle Oil:** Stir in cheddar, Parmesan, truffle oil, salt, and pepper until melted and smooth.
4. **Combine:** Toss the cooked macaroni in the cheese sauce. If desired, top with breadcrumbs and broil for 2-3 minutes until golden.

Kale Caesar Salad with Parmesan Crisps

Ingredients:

- 1 bunch kale, chopped
- 1/4 cup olive oil
- 2 tablespoons lemon juice
- 1 clove garlic, minced
- 2 tablespoons Dijon mustard
- 1/4 cup grated Parmesan cheese
- Salt and pepper to taste

For Parmesan Crisps:

- 1/2 cup shredded Parmesan cheese

Instructions:

1. **Make Parmesan Crisps:** Preheat oven to 375°F (190°C). Line a baking sheet with parchment paper. Place small mounds of shredded Parmesan on the sheet and flatten. Bake for 5-7 minutes until golden and crispy.
2. **Prepare Dressing:** In a small bowl, whisk olive oil, lemon juice, garlic, Dijon mustard, and Parmesan cheese. Season with salt and pepper.
3. **Assemble Salad:** Toss the kale with the dressing and top with Parmesan crisps.

Avocado Toast with Poached Egg and Pesto

Ingredients:

- 2 slices sourdough bread, toasted
- 1 ripe avocado, mashed
- 2 eggs, poached
- 2 tablespoons pesto
- Salt and pepper to taste

Instructions:

1. **Prepare the Toast:** Spread mashed avocado evenly over the toasted sourdough slices. Season with salt and pepper.
2. **Poach the Eggs:** Poach the eggs in simmering water for 3-4 minutes until the whites are set but the yolks remain runny.
3. **Assemble the Toast:** Place a poached egg on each slice of toast and drizzle with pesto.

Lobster Roll with Spicy Sriracha Mayo

Ingredients:

- 1 lb cooked lobster meat, chopped
- 4 hot dog buns, toasted
- 2 tablespoons mayonnaise
- 1 tablespoon Sriracha sauce
- 1 tablespoon lemon juice
- 2 tablespoons butter, melted
- Fresh chives for garnish

Instructions:

1. **Make Spicy Sriracha Mayo:** In a small bowl, mix mayonnaise, Sriracha, and lemon juice.
2. **Prepare Lobster Roll:** Toss the lobster meat with the melted butter and spicy mayo. Season with salt and pepper.
3. **Assemble the Roll:** Fill each toasted bun with the lobster mixture and garnish with fresh chives.

BBQ Pulled Pork Tacos with Pineapple Salsa

Ingredients:

- 1 lb pulled pork
- 8 small tortillas
- 1/2 cup BBQ sauce
- 1 cup pineapple, diced
- 1/4 cup red onion, diced
- 1/4 cup cilantro, chopped
- Juice of 1 lime

Instructions:

1. **Prepare the Pork:** Warm the pulled pork and mix with BBQ sauce.
2. **Make Pineapple Salsa:** In a bowl, combine pineapple, red onion, cilantro, and lime juice.
3. **Assemble the Tacos:** Fill tortillas with pulled pork and top with pineapple salsa.

Kimchi Grilled Cheese Sandwich

Ingredients:

- 4 slices sourdough bread
- 4 slices cheddar cheese
- 1/2 cup kimchi, drained and chopped
- 2 tablespoons butter

Instructions:

1. **Assemble the Sandwiches:** Layer cheese and kimchi between slices of bread.
2. **Grill the Sandwiches:** Heat a skillet over medium heat and melt butter. Grill sandwiches until bread is golden and cheese is melted, about 3-4 minutes per side.

Bison Burgers with Blue Cheese

Ingredients:

- 1 lb ground bison
- 1/4 cup blue cheese crumbles
- 4 burger buns
- 1 tablespoon Worcestershire sauce
- Salt and pepper to taste
- Lettuce, tomato, and onions for topping

Instructions:

1. **Make the Patties:** In a bowl, mix ground bison with Worcestershire sauce, salt, and pepper. Form into 4 patties.
2. **Cook the Burgers:** Grill or pan-fry the patties for 4-5 minutes per side until cooked to your desired doneness.
3. **Assemble the Burgers:** Place patties on buns, top with blue cheese, and add lettuce, tomato, and onions.

Enjoy these gourmet recipes!

Sweet Potato Fries with Chipotle Aioli

Ingredients:

- **For the Fries:**
    - 2 large sweet potatoes, peeled and cut into fries
    - 2 tablespoons olive oil
    - 1 teaspoon paprika
    - 1/2 teaspoon garlic powder
    - Salt and pepper to taste
- **For the Chipotle Aioli:**
    - 1/2 cup mayonnaise
    - 1 tablespoon lime juice
    - 1 chipotle pepper in adobo sauce, finely chopped
    - Salt to taste

Instructions:

1. **Prepare the Fries:** Preheat oven to 425°F (220°C). Toss sweet potato fries with olive oil, paprika, garlic powder, salt, and pepper. Spread on a baking sheet and bake for 25-30 minutes, flipping halfway through, until crispy.
2. **Make the Chipotle Aioli:** In a small bowl, mix mayonnaise, lime juice, chipotle pepper, and salt. Serve with the sweet potato fries.

Cauliflower Crust Pizza with Arugula

Ingredients:

- **For the Crust:**
    - 1 head cauliflower, grated
    - 1 egg
    - 1/2 cup mozzarella cheese, shredded
    - 1/4 cup Parmesan cheese, grated
    - 1/2 teaspoon oregano
    - Salt and pepper to taste
- **For the Toppings:**
    - 1/2 cup marinara sauce
    - 1/2 cup mozzarella cheese, shredded
    - 1 cup fresh arugula
    - 1 tablespoon olive oil
    - 1/2 teaspoon lemon juice

Instructions:

1. **Make the Crust:** Preheat oven to 400°F (200°C). Microwave grated cauliflower for 5 minutes, then squeeze out excess moisture. Mix cauliflower with egg, cheeses, oregano, salt, and pepper. Spread onto a parchment-lined baking sheet and bake for 20 minutes.
2. **Assemble the Pizza:** Spread marinara sauce on the crust, top with mozzarella cheese, and bake for another 10 minutes. Toss arugula with olive oil and lemon juice, and top the pizza before serving.

Miso-Glazed Salmon with Quinoa

Ingredients:

- 4 salmon fillets
- 2 tablespoons miso paste
- 1 tablespoon soy sauce
- 1 tablespoon honey
- 1 tablespoon rice vinegar
- 1 cup quinoa, cooked
- 1 tablespoon sesame seeds
- 2 green onions, sliced

Instructions:

1. **Prepare the Salmon:** Preheat oven to 400°F (200°C). In a bowl, whisk together miso paste, soy sauce, honey, and rice vinegar. Brush the mixture over the salmon fillets.
2. **Bake the Salmon:** Place salmon on a baking sheet and bake for 12-15 minutes until cooked through.
3. **Serve:** Serve the miso-glazed salmon over quinoa and garnish with sesame seeds and sliced green onions.

Buffalo Cauliflower Wings

Ingredients:

- 1 head cauliflower, cut into florets
- 1/2 cup flour
- 1/2 cup water
- 1/2 teaspoon garlic powder
- 1/2 cup hot sauce
- 2 tablespoons butter, melted
- Ranch dressing for dipping

Instructions:

1. **Prepare the Cauliflower:** Preheat oven to 425°F (220°C). In a bowl, mix flour, water, and garlic powder to make a batter. Toss cauliflower florets in the batter, then spread on a baking sheet.
2. **Bake the Cauliflower:** Bake for 20-25 minutes until golden and crispy.
3. **Toss in Buffalo Sauce:** In a small bowl, mix hot sauce and melted butter. Toss baked cauliflower in the buffalo sauce and serve with ranch dressing.

Pumpkin-Spiced French Toast

Ingredients:

- 4 slices of bread
- 2 eggs
- 1/2 cup milk
- 1/4 cup pumpkin puree
- 1 teaspoon pumpkin spice
- 1 tablespoon maple syrup
- Butter for cooking

Instructions:

1. **Make the Batter:** In a bowl, whisk together eggs, milk, pumpkin puree, pumpkin spice, and maple syrup.
2. **Cook the French Toast:** Dip each slice of bread in the batter and cook in a buttered skillet over medium heat for 2-3 minutes per side until golden.
3. **Serve:** Serve the French toast with a drizzle of maple syrup and extra pumpkin spice if desired.

Spaghetti Carbonara with Zucchini Noodles

Ingredients:

- 4 zucchinis, spiralized
- 4 slices bacon, chopped
- 2 eggs
- 1/2 cup Parmesan cheese, grated
- 1 clove garlic, minced
- Salt and pepper to taste

Instructions:

1. **Cook the Bacon:** In a skillet, cook bacon over medium heat until crispy. Remove from the skillet, leaving some bacon fat behind.
2. **Cook the Zucchini Noodles:** Add garlic to the skillet and sauté for 1 minute. Add zucchini noodles and cook for 2-3 minutes until slightly softened.
3. **Make the Sauce:** In a bowl, whisk eggs and Parmesan cheese together. Remove the skillet from heat and toss the zucchini noodles with the egg mixture. Add bacon and season with salt and pepper.

Vegan Chocolate Avocado Mousse

Ingredients:

- 2 ripe avocados
- 1/4 cup cocoa powder
- 1/4 cup almond milk
- 1/4 cup maple syrup
- 1 teaspoon vanilla extract
- Pinch of salt

Instructions:

1. **Blend the Ingredients:** In a blender or food processor, combine avocados, cocoa powder, almond milk, maple syrup, vanilla extract, and salt. Blend until smooth and creamy.
2. **Chill and Serve:** Spoon the mousse into serving dishes and chill for at least 30 minutes before serving.

Enjoy these vibrant and flavorful dishes!

Coconut Milk Pancakes

Ingredients:

- 1 1/2 cups all-purpose flour
- 2 tablespoons sugar
- 1 tablespoon baking powder
- 1/2 teaspoon salt
- 1 cup coconut milk
- 2 eggs
- 2 tablespoons melted butter
- 1 teaspoon vanilla extract
- Butter or oil for cooking

Instructions:

1. **Prepare the Batter:** In a bowl, whisk together flour, sugar, baking powder, and salt. In a separate bowl, mix coconut milk, eggs, melted butter, and vanilla extract. Combine the wet and dry ingredients until smooth.
2. **Cook the Pancakes:** Heat a non-stick skillet or griddle over medium heat and grease with butter or oil. Pour batter onto the skillet and cook for 2-3 minutes on each side until golden brown. Serve with syrup or fresh fruit.

Tuna Poke Bowl with Brown Rice

Ingredients:

- 1 cup brown rice, cooked
- 1/2 lb sushi-grade tuna, diced
- 1 avocado, diced
- 1/2 cup cucumber, sliced
- 2 tablespoons soy sauce
- 1 tablespoon sesame oil
- 1 teaspoon rice vinegar
- 1 tablespoon sesame seeds
- Green onions, chopped

Instructions:

1. **Prepare the Tuna:** In a small bowl, mix soy sauce, sesame oil, and rice vinegar. Toss the diced tuna in the mixture and set aside to marinate for 10 minutes.
2. **Assemble the Poke Bowl:** In a bowl, place cooked brown rice as the base. Top with marinated tuna, avocado, cucumber, sesame seeds, and green onions.

Spinach Artichoke Dip with Roasted Red Peppers

Ingredients:

- 1 cup spinach, cooked and drained
- 1 can artichoke hearts, chopped
- 1/2 cup roasted red peppers, chopped
- 1 cup cream cheese, softened
- 1/2 cup sour cream
- 1/2 cup mozzarella cheese, shredded
- 1/4 cup Parmesan cheese, grated
- Salt and pepper to taste

Instructions:

1. **Mix the Ingredients:** In a bowl, combine cream cheese, sour cream, spinach, artichokes, roasted red peppers, mozzarella, Parmesan, salt, and pepper.
2. **Bake the Dip:** Preheat oven to 350°F (175°C). Transfer the mixture to a baking dish and bake for 20-25 minutes until bubbly and golden. Serve with crackers or bread.

Duck Confit Tacos with Mango Salsa

Ingredients:

- 2 cups duck confit, shredded
- 8 small tortillas
- 1 cup mango, diced
- 1/4 cup red onion, diced
- 1 tablespoon lime juice
- 1 tablespoon cilantro, chopped
- Salt and pepper to taste

Instructions:

1. **Prepare the Mango Salsa:** In a bowl, mix mango, red onion, lime juice, cilantro, salt, and pepper. Set aside.
2. **Assemble the Tacos:** Warm the tortillas and fill each with shredded duck confit. Top with mango salsa and serve.

Sweet and Spicy Korean Fried Chicken

Ingredients:

- 1 lb chicken wings
- 1/2 cup cornstarch
- 1/2 cup flour
- 1/2 teaspoon garlic powder
- 1/2 teaspoon ginger powder
- 1/4 cup gochujang (Korean chili paste)
- 2 tablespoons honey
- 1 tablespoon soy sauce
- 1 tablespoon rice vinegar
- Vegetable oil for frying

Instructions:

1. **Prepare the Chicken:** In a bowl, mix cornstarch, flour, garlic powder, and ginger powder. Dredge chicken wings in the mixture.
2. **Fry the Chicken:** Heat vegetable oil in a deep skillet or fryer. Fry the chicken wings for 8-10 minutes until golden and crispy.
3. **Make the Sauce:** In a separate bowl, mix gochujang, honey, soy sauce, and rice vinegar. Toss the fried chicken wings in the sauce and serve.

Lamb Meatballs with Mint Yogurt Sauce

Ingredients:

- **For the Meatballs:**
    - 1 lb ground lamb
    - 1/4 cup breadcrumbs
    - 1 egg
    - 1 teaspoon cumin
    - 1 clove garlic, minced
    - Salt and pepper to taste
- **For the Mint Yogurt Sauce:**
    - 1/2 cup plain Greek yogurt
    - 1 tablespoon mint, chopped
    - 1 tablespoon lemon juice
    - Salt to taste

Instructions:

1. **Prepare the Meatballs:** In a bowl, combine ground lamb, breadcrumbs, egg, cumin, garlic, salt, and pepper. Form into small meatballs.
2. **Cook the Meatballs:** Heat oil in a skillet over medium heat and cook meatballs for 8-10 minutes, turning occasionally until browned and cooked through.
3. **Make the Mint Yogurt Sauce:** In a small bowl, mix Greek yogurt, mint, lemon juice, and salt. Serve the meatballs with the yogurt sauce.

Chickpea Pasta with Roasted Vegetables

Ingredients:

- 8 oz chickpea pasta
- 1 cup cherry tomatoes, halved
- 1 zucchini, diced
- 1 red bell pepper, chopped
- 2 tablespoons olive oil
- 1 teaspoon garlic powder
- Salt and pepper to taste
- 1/4 cup Parmesan cheese, grated (optional)

Instructions:

1. **Roast the Vegetables:** Preheat oven to 400°F (200°C). Toss tomatoes, zucchini, and bell pepper with olive oil, garlic powder, salt, and pepper. Spread on a baking sheet and roast for 20-25 minutes.
2. **Cook the Pasta:** Cook chickpea pasta according to package instructions. Drain and toss with roasted vegetables. Serve with Parmesan cheese if desired.

Enjoy these globally inspired, flavor-packed dishes!

Charred Brussels Sprouts with Balsamic Glaze

Ingredients:

- 1 lb Brussels sprouts, halved
- 2 tablespoons olive oil
- Salt and pepper to taste
- 1/4 cup balsamic vinegar
- 1 tablespoon honey

Instructions:

1. **Cook the Brussels Sprouts:** Heat olive oil in a skillet over medium-high heat. Add Brussels sprouts, cut side down, and cook for 4-5 minutes until charred and crispy. Season with salt and pepper.
2. **Make the Balsamic Glaze:** In a small saucepan, reduce balsamic vinegar and honey over low heat until thickened. Drizzle over the Brussels sprouts and serve.

Sriracha Honey Roasted Carrots

Ingredients:

- 1 lb carrots, peeled and sliced
- 2 tablespoons olive oil
- 1 tablespoon sriracha
- 2 tablespoons honey
- Salt and pepper to taste

Instructions:

1. **Roast the Carrots:** Preheat oven to 400°F (200°C). Toss carrots with olive oil, sriracha, honey, salt, and pepper. Spread on a baking sheet and roast for 25-30 minutes until tender and caramelized.
2. **Serve:** Remove from the oven and serve warm.

Gourmet Grilled Cheese with Apple Slices

Ingredients:

- 4 slices sourdough bread
- 2 tablespoons butter
- 4 slices sharp cheddar cheese
- 1 apple, thinly sliced
- 1 tablespoon Dijon mustard

Instructions:

1. **Assemble the Sandwiches:** Spread Dijon mustard on two slices of bread. Layer each with cheddar cheese and apple slices, and top with the remaining bread slices.
2. **Cook the Grilled Cheese:** Heat butter in a skillet over medium heat. Grill the sandwiches for 3-4 minutes per side until golden brown and the cheese is melted. Serve hot.

Sous Vide Steak with Chimichurri

Ingredients:

- 2 ribeye steaks
- Salt and pepper to taste
- 2 tablespoons olive oil
- **For the Chimichurri Sauce:**
    - 1/2 cup parsley, chopped
    - 1/4 cup olive oil
    - 2 tablespoons red wine vinegar
    - 1 garlic clove, minced
    - 1 teaspoon red pepper flakes
    - Salt and pepper to taste

Instructions:

1. **Sous Vide the Steak:** Season steaks with salt and pepper, then seal them in a vacuum bag. Cook sous vide at 130°F (54°C) for 1-2 hours.
2. **Sear the Steak:** Heat olive oil in a skillet over high heat and sear the steaks for 1 minute per side.
3. **Make the Chimichurri:** In a small bowl, mix parsley, olive oil, red wine vinegar, garlic, red pepper flakes, salt, and pepper. Serve the steak with chimichurri sauce.

Greek Yogurt Parfait with Granola and Fresh Berries

Ingredients:

- 1 cup Greek yogurt
- 1/2 cup granola
- 1/2 cup fresh berries (strawberries, blueberries, raspberries)
- 1 tablespoon honey

Instructions:

1. **Assemble the Parfait:** Layer Greek yogurt, granola, and fresh berries in a glass. Drizzle with honey.
2. **Serve:** Repeat layers as desired and serve immediately.

Quinoa-Stuffed Bell Peppers

Ingredients:

- 4 bell peppers, tops removed and seeds scooped out
- 1 cup cooked quinoa
- 1/2 cup black beans
- 1/2 cup corn kernels
- 1/4 cup diced tomatoes
- 1/4 cup shredded cheese (optional)
- Salt and pepper to taste

Instructions:

1. **Prepare the Filling:** In a bowl, mix cooked quinoa, black beans, corn, tomatoes, salt, and pepper. Stuff the mixture into the bell peppers.
2. **Bake the Peppers:** Preheat oven to 375°F (190°C). Place stuffed peppers in a baking dish and bake for 25-30 minutes. Top with cheese, if desired, and bake for another 5 minutes.

Crispy Duck Breast with Orange Glaze

Ingredients:

- 2 duck breasts, scored
- Salt and pepper to taste
- 1/4 cup orange juice
- 2 tablespoons honey
- 1 tablespoon soy sauce
- 1 tablespoon balsamic vinegar

Instructions:

1. **Cook the Duck Breast:** Season duck breasts with salt and pepper. Place them skin-side down in a cold skillet and cook over medium heat for 6-8 minutes until the skin is crispy. Flip and cook for another 4-5 minutes. Remove from the skillet and rest.
2. **Make the Orange Glaze:** In the same skillet, combine orange juice, honey, soy sauce, and balsamic vinegar. Simmer until reduced and thickened.
3. **Serve:** Slice the duck breast and drizzle with orange glaze.

Enjoy these flavorful dishes!

Tiramisu Ice Cream Sandwiches

Ingredients:

- 12 ladyfingers
- 2 cups coffee-flavored ice cream
- 1 tablespoon cocoa powder
- 1 tablespoon espresso, brewed and cooled
- 1/4 cup mascarpone cheese
- 1/2 teaspoon vanilla extract

Instructions:

1. **Prepare Filling:** In a bowl, mix the mascarpone cheese, vanilla extract, and espresso. Set aside.
2. **Assemble the Sandwiches:** Spread a layer of coffee ice cream on the flat side of six ladyfingers. Top with the mascarpone mixture and another ladyfinger to create sandwiches.
3. **Freeze:** Place sandwiches on a tray and freeze for 1-2 hours. Before serving, dust with cocoa powder.

Spaghetti Squash Alfredo

Ingredients:

- 1 large spaghetti squash
- 1/2 cup heavy cream
- 1/4 cup Parmesan cheese, grated
- 2 garlic cloves, minced
- 1 tablespoon butter
- Salt and pepper to taste
- Fresh parsley for garnish

Instructions:

1. **Cook the Squash:** Preheat oven to 400°F (200°C). Cut spaghetti squash in half, remove seeds, and bake for 40-45 minutes until tender. Scrape the flesh into strands.
2. **Make the Alfredo Sauce:** In a saucepan, melt butter over medium heat. Add garlic and cook for 1 minute. Stir in heavy cream and Parmesan cheese, then season with salt and pepper.
3. **Combine and Serve:** Toss the spaghetti squash with the Alfredo sauce and garnish with parsley.

Grilled Corn Salad with Feta and Lime

Ingredients:

- 4 ears of corn, grilled and kernels removed
- 1/4 cup feta cheese, crumbled
- 1/4 cup red onion, diced
- 2 tablespoons lime juice
- 1 tablespoon olive oil
- Salt and pepper to taste
- Fresh cilantro for garnish

Instructions:

1. **Make the Salad:** In a large bowl, combine grilled corn, feta, red onion, lime juice, olive oil, salt, and pepper.
2. **Serve:** Toss the salad and garnish with cilantro before serving.

Matcha Green Tea Cheesecake

Ingredients:

- 1 1/2 cups graham cracker crumbs
- 1/4 cup melted butter
- 16 oz cream cheese, softened
- 1/2 cup sugar
- 2 tablespoons matcha powder
- 2 eggs
- 1 teaspoon vanilla extract

Instructions:

1. **Make the Crust:** Preheat oven to 325°F (160°C). Mix graham cracker crumbs with melted butter and press into a springform pan.
2. **Prepare Filling:** Beat cream cheese, sugar, matcha powder, eggs, and vanilla until smooth. Pour over the crust.
3. **Bake:** Bake for 40-45 minutes. Let cool and refrigerate before serving.

Shrimp Scampi with Zoodles

Ingredients:

- 1 lb shrimp, peeled and deveined
- 4 zucchini, spiralized
- 3 garlic cloves, minced
- 1/4 cup white wine
- 2 tablespoons butter
- 2 tablespoons lemon juice
- Salt, pepper, and red pepper flakes to taste
- Fresh parsley for garnish

Instructions:

1. **Cook the Shrimp:** In a large skillet, melt butter and sauté garlic for 1 minute. Add shrimp and cook until pink, about 3-4 minutes.
2. **Add Wine and Lemon Juice:** Pour in white wine and lemon juice, simmering for 2 minutes. Season with salt, pepper, and red pepper flakes.
3. **Add Zoodles:** Toss in the zucchini noodles and cook for 2-3 minutes. Garnish with parsley and serve.

Slow-Cooked Short Ribs with Gremolata

Ingredients:

- 4 lbs beef short ribs
- 1 onion, diced
- 3 garlic cloves, minced
- 2 cups beef broth
- 1/4 cup red wine
- 2 tablespoons tomato paste
- Salt and pepper to taste
- **For the Gremolata:**
    - 1/4 cup parsley, chopped
    - 1 tablespoon lemon zest
    - 1 garlic clove, minced

Instructions:

1. **Slow-Cook the Ribs:** In a slow cooker, combine short ribs, onion, garlic, beef broth, red wine, and tomato paste. Season with salt and pepper. Cook on low for 8 hours.
2. **Make the Gremolata:** Mix parsley, lemon zest, and garlic in a small bowl.
3. **Serve:** Top the cooked short ribs with gremolata before serving.

Tomato Soup with Grilled Cheese Croutons

Ingredients:

- 4 large tomatoes, chopped
- 1 onion, diced
- 2 garlic cloves, minced
- 1 tablespoon olive oil
- 2 cups vegetable broth
- Salt and pepper to taste
- 4 slices of bread
- 2 tablespoons butter
- 4 slices cheddar cheese

Instructions:

1. **Make the Soup:** In a large pot, sauté onion and garlic in olive oil until softened. Add tomatoes and broth, and simmer for 20 minutes. Blend until smooth and season with salt and pepper.
2. **Make Grilled Cheese Croutons:** Butter bread slices, place cheese between them, and grill until golden. Cut into croutons.
3. **Serve:** Ladle soup into bowls and top with grilled cheese croutons.

Enjoy these delicious dishes!

Sourdough Pizza with Prosciutto and Arugula

Ingredients:

- 1 sourdough pizza crust
- 1/2 cup pizza sauce
- 1 1/2 cups mozzarella cheese, shredded
- 4 slices prosciutto
- 1 cup fresh arugula
- 1 tablespoon olive oil
- Salt and pepper to taste

Instructions:

1. **Prepare the Pizza:** Preheat oven to 475°F (245°C). Spread pizza sauce over the sourdough crust, then sprinkle mozzarella cheese on top.
2. **Bake:** Place prosciutto slices on the pizza and bake for 10-12 minutes until cheese is bubbly and crust is golden.
3. **Top and Serve:** Remove from oven, top with arugula, drizzle with olive oil, and season with salt and pepper.

Chili Lime Roasted Chickpeas

Ingredients:

- 1 can chickpeas, drained and rinsed
- 1 tablespoon olive oil
- 1 teaspoon chili powder
- 1/2 teaspoon cumin
- 1 tablespoon lime juice
- Salt to taste

Instructions:

1. **Season the Chickpeas:** Preheat oven to 400°F (200°C). Toss chickpeas with olive oil, chili powder, cumin, lime juice, and salt.
2. **Roast:** Spread chickpeas on a baking sheet and roast for 25-30 minutes until crispy. Stir halfway through.
3. **Serve:** Let cool slightly and serve as a crunchy snack.

Eggplant Parmesan with Mozzarella and Pesto

Ingredients:

- 2 large eggplants, sliced
- 1 cup marinara sauce
- 1 cup mozzarella cheese, shredded
- 1/4 cup pesto
- 1/4 cup Parmesan cheese, grated
- Olive oil for frying
- Salt and pepper to taste

Instructions:

1. **Cook the Eggplant:** Preheat oven to 375°F (190°C). Fry eggplant slices in olive oil until golden and soft. Drain on paper towels and season with salt.
2. **Assemble and Bake:** In a baking dish, layer fried eggplant, marinara sauce, mozzarella, and pesto. Top with Parmesan and bake for 25 minutes.
3. **Serve:** Let cool slightly before serving.

Crab Cakes with Avocado-Lime Sauce

Ingredients:

- 1 lb crabmeat
- 1/4 cup breadcrumbs
- 1 egg, beaten
- 2 tablespoons mayo
- 1 tablespoon Dijon mustard
- 1 tablespoon lemon juice
- **For the Avocado-Lime Sauce:**
    - 1 ripe avocado
    - 1 tablespoon lime juice
    - Salt and pepper to taste

Instructions:

1. **Make the Crab Cakes:** In a bowl, mix crabmeat, breadcrumbs, egg, mayo, Dijon mustard, and lemon juice. Form into patties.
2. **Cook:** Heat a skillet with oil and fry the crab cakes until golden, about 3-4 minutes per side.
3. **Make the Sauce:** Blend avocado, lime juice, salt, and pepper until smooth. Serve crab cakes with the avocado-lime sauce.

Avocado Chocolate Chip Cookies

Ingredients:

- 1 ripe avocado, mashed
- 1/2 cup brown sugar
- 1/4 cup coconut oil
- 1 egg
- 1 teaspoon vanilla extract
- 1 1/4 cups flour
- 1/2 teaspoon baking soda
- 1/2 teaspoon salt
- 1/2 cup chocolate chips

Instructions:

1. **Prepare the Dough:** Preheat oven to 350°F (175°C). In a bowl, mix mashed avocado, brown sugar, coconut oil, egg, and vanilla. Stir in flour, baking soda, and salt. Fold in chocolate chips.
2. **Bake:** Drop spoonfuls of dough onto a baking sheet and bake for 10-12 minutes until edges are golden.
3. **Cool and Serve:** Let cool before serving.

Grilled Watermelon Salad with Feta

Ingredients:

- 4 watermelon slices
- 1/4 cup feta cheese, crumbled
- 2 tablespoons balsamic glaze
- 1 tablespoon olive oil
- Fresh mint leaves for garnish
- Salt and pepper to taste

Instructions:

1. **Grill the Watermelon:** Heat grill to medium-high. Lightly brush watermelon slices with olive oil and grill for 2-3 minutes per side.
2. **Assemble the Salad:** Arrange grilled watermelon on a plate, top with feta, drizzle with balsamic glaze, and season with salt and pepper.
3. **Garnish and Serve:** Garnish with fresh mint leaves and serve immediately.

Gluten-Free Banana Bread with Almond Flour

Ingredients:

- 2 cups almond flour
- 2 ripe bananas, mashed
- 2 eggs
- 1/4 cup honey
- 1 teaspoon baking powder
- 1 teaspoon cinnamon
- 1/2 teaspoon vanilla extract

Instructions:

1. **Prepare the Batter:** Preheat oven to 350°F (175°C). In a bowl, mix mashed bananas, eggs, honey, cinnamon, and vanilla. Add almond flour and baking powder, stirring until smooth.
2. **Bake:** Pour the batter into a greased loaf pan and bake for 45-50 minutes until golden and cooked through.
3. **Cool and Serve:** Let cool before slicing and serving.

Enjoy making and tasting these delicious recipes!

Spicy Thai Peanut Noodles

Ingredients:

- 8 oz rice noodles
- 1/4 cup peanut butter
- 2 tablespoons soy sauce
- 1 tablespoon lime juice
- 1 tablespoon sriracha
- 1 tablespoon sesame oil
- 1 garlic clove, minced
- 1/2 cup carrots, julienned
- 1/2 cup bell peppers, sliced
- Chopped peanuts and cilantro for garnish

Instructions:

1. **Cook the Noodles:** Prepare noodles according to package instructions, then drain and set aside.
2. **Make the Sauce:** In a bowl, whisk together peanut butter, soy sauce, lime juice, sriracha, sesame oil, and garlic.
3. **Combine:** Toss the cooked noodles with the peanut sauce, then add carrots and bell peppers.
4. **Serve:** Garnish with chopped peanuts and cilantro.

Lobster Mac and Cheese

Ingredients:

- 8 oz elbow macaroni
- 2 lobster tails, cooked and chopped
- 2 cups sharp cheddar cheese, shredded
- 1 cup Gruyere cheese, shredded
- 2 cups milk
- 3 tablespoons butter
- 3 tablespoons flour
- 1/2 cup breadcrumbs
- Salt and pepper to taste

Instructions:

1. **Cook the Pasta:** Prepare macaroni according to package instructions, drain, and set aside.
2. **Make the Cheese Sauce:** In a pot, melt butter and stir in flour. Gradually add milk, stirring until thickened. Add cheddar and Gruyere cheeses, salt, and pepper. Stir until smooth.
3. **Combine and Bake:** Mix the cooked pasta and lobster into the cheese sauce, transfer to a baking dish, top with breadcrumbs, and bake at 350°F (175°C) for 20 minutes.

Smoked Salmon Eggs Benedict on Sweet Potato Toast

Ingredients:

- 2 sweet potatoes, sliced into 1/2-inch pieces
- 4 poached eggs
- 4 oz smoked salmon
- 1/2 cup hollandaise sauce
- Salt and pepper to taste
- Fresh dill for garnish

Instructions:

1. **Prepare Sweet Potato Toast:** Preheat oven to 400°F (200°C). Roast sweet potato slices for 20 minutes until tender and golden.
2. **Assemble:** Top each sweet potato slice with smoked salmon and a poached egg. Drizzle with hollandaise sauce.
3. **Garnish:** Season with salt, pepper, and garnish with fresh dill.

Buffalo Chicken Stuffed Sweet Potatoes

Ingredients:

- 4 medium sweet potatoes
- 2 cups shredded cooked chicken
- 1/4 cup buffalo sauce
- 1/4 cup ranch dressing
- 1/2 cup shredded cheddar cheese
- Green onions for garnish

Instructions:

1. **Bake the Sweet Potatoes:** Preheat oven to 400°F (200°C). Pierce sweet potatoes and bake for 45 minutes until tender.
2. **Prepare the Filling:** In a bowl, mix shredded chicken with buffalo sauce.
3. **Assemble:** Cut open each sweet potato, stuff with buffalo chicken, top with cheese, and drizzle with ranch dressing. Garnish with green onions.

Lemon Ricotta Pancakes with Berries

Ingredients:

- 1 cup ricotta cheese
- 1 cup flour
- 1 tablespoon sugar
- 1 teaspoon baking powder
- 2 eggs, separated
- 3/4 cup milk
- 1 tablespoon lemon zest
- Fresh berries for serving
- Maple syrup for serving

Instructions:

1. **Prepare the Batter:** In a bowl, whisk together ricotta, egg yolks, milk, lemon zest, and sugar. Fold in flour and baking powder. Beat egg whites until stiff peaks form and fold into the batter.
2. **Cook the Pancakes:** Heat a skillet over medium heat and cook the batter in batches until golden.
3. **Serve:** Top with fresh berries and drizzle with maple syrup.

Grilled Portobello Mushroom Burgers

Ingredients:

- 4 large portobello mushrooms
- 4 burger buns
- 2 tablespoons balsamic vinegar
- 2 tablespoons olive oil
- 1 tablespoon soy sauce
- 4 slices provolone cheese
- Lettuce, tomato, and onion for serving

Instructions:

1. **Marinate the Mushrooms:** In a bowl, whisk together balsamic vinegar, olive oil, and soy sauce. Marinate the mushrooms for 20 minutes.
2. **Grill the Mushrooms:** Heat the grill and cook mushrooms for 5-7 minutes per side. Top with provolone cheese during the last minute.
3. **Assemble:** Serve on buns with lettuce, tomato, and onion.

Roasted Cauliflower Steaks with Chimichurri

Ingredients:

- 1 large cauliflower, sliced into steaks
- 2 tablespoons olive oil
- Salt and pepper to taste
- **For Chimichurri:**
    - 1/2 cup parsley
    - 2 garlic cloves
    - 2 tablespoons red wine vinegar
    - 1/4 cup olive oil
    - 1/2 teaspoon red pepper flakes

Instructions:

1. **Roast the Cauliflower:** Preheat oven to 425°F (220°C). Drizzle cauliflower steaks with olive oil, season with salt and pepper, and roast for 25 minutes until golden.
2. **Make the Chimichurri:** Blend all chimichurri ingredients together until smooth.
3. **Serve:** Drizzle the roasted cauliflower steaks with chimichurri sauce.

Chocolate Chip Skillet Cookie with Sea Salt

Ingredients:

- 1/2 cup butter, melted
- 1/2 cup brown sugar
- 1/4 cup granulated sugar
- 1 egg
- 1 teaspoon vanilla extract
- 1 1/4 cups flour
- 1/2 teaspoon baking soda
- 1/2 teaspoon salt
- 1 cup chocolate chips
- Sea salt for garnish

Instructions:

1. **Prepare the Dough:** Preheat oven to 350°F (175°C). In a skillet, mix melted butter, brown sugar, and granulated sugar. Stir in egg and vanilla. Add flour, baking soda, and salt, mixing until smooth. Fold in chocolate chips.
2. **Bake:** Bake in the skillet for 20-25 minutes until golden.
3. **Serve:** Sprinkle with sea salt and serve warm.

Enjoy making and savoring these delightful recipes!

www.ingramcontent.com/pod-product-compliance
Lightning Source LLC
LaVergne TN
LVHW081333060526
838201LV00055B/2626